To: Mi... God is always with you! Love You (handwritten inscription)

UNSHAKEABLE FAITH

A True Story of Triumph Over Tragedy
by Trusting God

Gloria Roberts-Lenear

Gloria Roberts-Lenear (signature)

Copyright Page

Dedication

I dedicate my story to those of you who have experienced multiple losses, who continue to struggle with moving forward and living their best life one day at a time. Those trusting God to walk with you through all times even when you are scared, unsure and don't have any idea of outcomes. I call it the "walk of faith."

Contents

Acknowledgements

I'd like to acknowledge and thank these people for their support on my journey.

First, I give honor to God. Next, I want to thank my son Paul Davis for his encouragement in me writing my story and introducing me to Dayna Mason. Dayna has been an extraordinary support in leading me through this entire process. She has guided me in how to put words on paper and this book wouldn't be in existence without her expertise and support. Thank you from my heart.

I'm also grateful for the love and support from all my adult children, my neice C'Ardiss who said, "You must write your story auntie." and from two dear sister friends Terry Green Johnson, and Teresa Banks who have walked me through most of my adversities for over thirty years being there every step of the way. I am truly grateful for their faithful sisterhood and friendship.

Lastly, I must thank my brother Michael Parker who has stood by me since childhood. Michael and I were extremely close growing up. He had my back through every adversity I faced and continues to stand with me today. Michael and I are the only two siblings remaining out of six.

Introduction

"Cast your cares on the Lord and He will sustain you." (Psalms 55:22)

Do you believe that God will not put more on you than you can bear? Do you really believe it? If so, how do you cope with trauma, tragedies, and the unexpected bumps in the road?

Do you give in or do you hold on to your faith in God and His Word? Do you have unshakable faith? Do you trust God no matter what you face? Is there anything too big for God to handle?

Come along with me as I share my personal journey of real-life challenges, tragedies, and despair, which I experienced from age four to the present day. More importantly, learn how God brought me through every single heart-wrenching experience through His Grace, and with my faith and determination.

Faith Sustained Me. No, Really. It Did.

Never give up! Your healing and blessings are always near!

Unshakeable Faith

Chapter 1

LEARNING TO TRUST GOD

*"Trust in the Lord with all your heart,
and do not lean on your own understanding."*

(Proverbs 3:5)

I was born and raised in the Yesler Terrace housing projects in Seattle's Central District, where most black folks resided in Washington state in the 1950s and '60s. A happy kid, I loved on people and wanted everyone to be kind to one another.

When I was four years old, my dad abandoned us, leaving my mom with four boys and two girls to raise as a single parent. Nights were the most difficult for me. I was terrified that someone would break into our house. Without my dad being in the home, I felt less protected because in my mind a man's physical strength provided safety.

I'd heard horror stories about racism and being a little "colored" girl. The TV news showed black folks being targeted by hatred and bigotry. I saw them water-hosed, spit on, hit by hurling rocks, yelled at with curse words, and I witnessed these evil acts being perpetrated by the angry faces of white people.

In kindergarten I attended Bailey Gatzert Elementary School. As a five-year-old, I often walked to school by myself, except on days when I was feeling especially afraid of the dogs in the neighborhood. Then my mom would walk with me past the neighborhood where dogs lived. I would walk the rest of the way alone.

I was an anxious kid and frequently had catastrophizing thoughts. My thoughts often overwhelmed my mind. I worried about so many things: my mom's poor health, fear of her early death, and not feeling safe in our home at night. Yet my prayers taught to me by my mother helped me believe that God was always with me and I had nothing to fear. The frightened little girl voice in my mind was full of frantic thoughts that consumed me at times. But there was the "still small voice" always reminding me "I will never leave you." I constantly struggled with which voice to listen to.

One Saturday morning my mom announced we were going to move to Rockford, Illinois, in hopes of reconciling with my dad. We packed up some clothing and snacks (fried chicken, oranges, and cookies). The rest of our things were sent ahead in huge trunks. We headed for the train station—the Empire Builder train. It was extremely cold in the Midwest. I didn't like anything about Rockford.

Six months after we arrived, once school was out for the year, my family headed to Fort Worth, Texas, for the summer to visit my grandmother, who had a huge farm.

The year was 1956 and Grandma had a big house with no electricity. When I needed to use the toilet, one of my brothers would escort me to the outhouse, which was a nightmare because it was pitch black outside at night and there were many scary sounds coming from the woods. I didn't know what was lurking out there in the dark, and the smell was horrible inside the outhouse. I had to hold my breath and it was difficult to sit on the wooden seat. I thought something was going to come up out of the hole and grab my private parts. And the hot weather only heightened the stench.

All my fears followed me from Seattle. I wondered if my heart would find calm in these new surroundings. I believed God was watching over me despite not being able to see him. I'd learned in Sunday school that faith, which is the "substance of things hoped for and evidence of things not seen" was all I needed to get by. There were times my mother was too sick to work, yet we had food on the table and a roof over our heads, which confirmed my trust in God.

Some meals consisted of corn meal mush, which was like a hot cereal. It was a horrible meal no matter how much butter, sugar, or fruit I added. The canned peaches were my saving grace and were added to most of our hot cereal for both breakfast and dinner. Yes, we had breakfast food for dinner often, as it was an easy meal to prepare. To this day, I still don't like hot cereal. But there was always food on the table, whether I enjoyed it or not. If I was hungry enough, I would eat whatever was placed in front of me.

The reconciliation of my mom and dad was not going well. I could hear them arguing in the middle of the night. My dad drank a clear liquid all the time that smelled strong. I wasn't sure what it was. It looked like water, but I was told it was gin or vodka. There were times during the day that Dad would take me and my siblings for a drive. Dad seemed happy when he was drinking. I could smell the strong odor in the car. In his highly spirited mood, when he walked in the store, Dad said to get whatever we wanted and yes, I did. I loved Hershey bars, Paydays, Milky Way bars, and Sugar Daddy's. Candy was only a nickel and a quarter went a long way in those times. I enjoyed the treats and looked forward to more treats. However, I was concerned about Dad's driving as he alternated between driving too fast and driving extremely slowly. My siblings often told him to slow down and watch the road, but I was preoccupied, munching on my candy.

The reconciliation of my parents didn't work out and we returned to Seattle, Washington, where we were enrolled in school before it started. We didn't return to Yesler Terrace; instead, we moved into a house at 3111 East Denny Street. How my mom managed that is beyond my imagination. A two-bedroom home for the seven of us. My mom and brothers had the luxury of the bedrooms, none of which were that big. My sister and I slept in the dining room in our beautiful mahogany bunk beds. I had the top bunk. There were no walls or doors protecting me at night. I would pull the covers over my head when I heard noises that sounded like someone breaking in either the front or back doors, or maybe coming up from the creepy unfinished basement. I repeated my prayers to help me fall asleep. I would wake my sister when I had to go to the toilet, even though the bathroom was indoors (unlike living with my grandma in the backwoods of Texas). I wanted my sister to know I was going to the bathroom in case something happened to me. I prayed as I headed to the bathroom. Often I prayed for God to protect me and my family. At seven years old I started first grade at Madrona Elementary School. I was happy to be back in Seattle and loved my school.

In 1959, at nine years old, my mom sent us to our neighbors, the Barnes family in Madison Valley, for Bible study. We also attended Union Gospel Mission Church. I enjoyed the summers and I attended Lake Sammamish Bible camp, where we sang around the campfire, roasted hot dogs and marshmallows, played competitive games, ran relay races, hiked, and swam. I liked sleeping in the cabins. I actually slept well while away at camp, knowing we were supervised. Often after lights were out, I would hear dirt bombs hitting the windows. Yes, it was the boys from the other side of the camp coming over to bother the girls. I was tickled and enjoyed the boys' silliness. Being raised with four brothers, I was comfortable around boys. But this Christian camp would challenge me around what I learned during Bible study, because my hormones were raging and that conflicted with the word of God. The Bible clearly defined what a male and female relationship should look like and I was much too young to be thinking about a relationship with a boy.

I felt I was too young to have feelings of excitement about boys. And I remembered the stories my mom shared about boys and men. "All they want is to get into your panties, get you pregnant, then leave for the next girl or woman." So I backed way off on how I interacted with boys. I became a tomboy. Also, I thought about my dad's relationship with my mom and I didn't want that for myself.

In 1960, at ten years old, the following summer, our family took a day trip to Cottage Lake for a picnic. We often had block parties during the summer where we would gather with our neighbors for a picnic and dance in the streets. This year the picnic moved away to Cottage Lake, where we could all go swimming, play games, and eat some good soul food. As soon as our mom gave the okay, we ran for the dressing rooms to change into our swimming suits.

While I was still in the process of putting my swimsuit on, I heard screams. "Help me! Help me! Help me!"

My siblings and I ran out of the dressing rooms and I realized it was our oldest brother Simmie, who was thirteen years old, and a lifeguard, screaming for help. He was caught in a whirlpool in the water, and there were men in a boat trying to rescue him. My brother was eventually pulled from the water and taken to Harborview Hospital, where he was pronounced dead upon arrival. This was tragic for everyone and my mom was never the same.

I will never forget my mom's grief. She withdrew from life. Often she would stay in her room, or she would sit at the dining room table, looking out the window with a blank stare on her face. This made me sad. I didn't want to go outside and play with my friends because I wanted to stay close to my mom. I was scared for her well-being and I began to withdraw from life, too. I didn't want to attend camp or take trips that would take me away from the house and leave my mom alone.

On the weekends, though, I often went to my big momma's house for time away from my siblings and to let her spoil me. She had a big house with a fenced-in backyard with fruit trees. She had a dog named Tuffy, who was part German Shepherd and part Collie. Normally I was petrified of dogs, but not Tuffy. He became my friend and I felt he would protect me if I needed protecting. I often went to church from big momma's house.

I lost myself in Sunday school at Mt. Zion Church, sometimes playing the piano and singing with the choir. I decided to get baptized at twelve years old. I was terrified of the water after witnessing my brother's drowning, but I was able to get baptized after fifteen minutes of encouragement. My love for singing God's praises kept me going. I would sing during my chores at home and would go out on the rooftop to sing "Oh How I Love Jesus," "What a Friend We Have in Jesus," and "How Great Thou Art." Singing was therapeutic and kept me calm in those anxious times.

Unshakeable Faith

Chapter 2

GOD SENDS PAUL

"Teach me good judgment and knowledge, for I believe in your commandments."

(Psalm 119:66)

When I was fourteen years old, we moved to 3212 East Terrace Street in Seattle's Leschi neighborhood, where my sister and I shared a large bedroom. I loved the rooftop outside our bedroom window because I felt it was my sanctuary, where I could go to sing, pray, and worship in my own way—alone, away from everyone. I could sing as loud as I wanted, and I pretended that I was on stage and ministering to the neighbors who might actually hear me. I would sing for hours and meditate quietly. I knew I was safe even in the dark because at any time, I could climb back inside my window.

I attended Washington Junior High School in the ninth grade, which went by quickly. I was enrolled in Garfield High School from tenth through twelfth grades. I was in the Choraleers Choir all three years in high school. As time passed, I became more connected to my faith in God and personal walk with Jesus Christ while attending Mt. Zion Church, Bible studies, programs, and outings with the Sunday school class. I felt a sense of peace and calmness in my spirit and was ready to take on more activities. I enjoyed traveling with the choir at church and in school. We would sing for different social events, and we were invited to sing at different churches in the community, where I met some nice people who added to my network of support.

No one could have prepared me for what was coming next in my life and what would be so traumatizing for years to come.

In 1966, at age sixteen, I attended a co-ed YWCA meeting group at 28th and Cherry streets. Our YWCA group had a bowling outing, where I met Paul, who was nineteen years old and home on leave from the military before heading out to Vietnam. He attempted to show me how to bowl properly. I thanked him and wished him well over in Vietnam. A week after that encounter, a friend of Paul's asked me if I would consider writing Paul while he was away in Vietnam. He said that Paul would like me to write him. I agreed and was happy to write letters to Paul to keep him apprised of what was happening here in Seattle. Each letter I wrote Paul drew us closer and closer together.

I needed to focus on my academics, but I found it difficult as my mind continually wandered off with thoughts of Paul. He was so handsome. I was also spending time with a dear friend, Stan, who looked out after me. We were the same age and in the same class. Stan was a kind young man and kept the bad guys away from me. We would go to the movies and drive-in together. My mom liked Stan and trusted him to take me to school and out on dates. I told Stan about Paul, but that didn't matter to him. He still wanted to hang out with me. Paul and I wrote to each other weekly and he also sent me two hand-painted pictures of the two of us. I hung them on my headboard. Paul's eyes mesmerized me and penetrated my soul.

The date was November 16, 1967. The telephone rang and my mom hollered up the stairs, "Jean, you have a long-distance call."

I ran down the stairs, almost tripping over my feet. "Hello," I said.

On the other end of the line was a sexy voice. "This is Paul. I'm in California."

I was in shock and pleasantly surprised. I knew he would be coming home soon but didn't know the exact date.

Paul said, "I'd like to come over and meet your mom and take you out to eat when I arrive in Seattle in two days."

I was delighted.

It was about six o'clock when he arrived at my house. I opened the door and stood there. When I finally gathered the words to speak and my heart stopped racing, I invited Paul in and introduced him to my mom.

We embraced and headed for IHOP (a pancake restaurant) on Madison Street near Broadway. I was so nervous, I couldn't eat. Eventually I calmed myself long enough to eat a pancake. Paul stared at me the entire time. He was eye candy. I was a looker, too. We talked about some of his experiences in Vietnam, the latest updates about happenings in Seattle, and his desire to get to know me better.

"Will you go with me?" Paul asked. This was the way you asked a girl to go steady with you.

"Yes!" I said, as he held my hand across the table. I was so excited. We finished our food and left the restaurant.

We took a drive around the Lake Washington waterfront, which was over the hill from my house. As he drove, we talked about the beauty of the lights and the moon shining down on the water and the beautiful waterfront homes. I still cherish this time with him today. As we returned to my house, Paul walked me up to the door and asked me for a kiss. Without thinking about it, I gave him a quick peck on his lips.

Paul said, "What was that? I want a real kiss."

He pulled me closer and gave me a kiss with his tongue. I pulled back.

"I don't do that," I said.

"Well, that's gonna change!" Paul said.

I smiled and proceeded into the house. I saw the dining room curtain move and realized my mom was watching us the entire time. I felt mortified because my Christian values were speaking to me. I was wondering what my mom was thinking of me, her daughter who was at this point so naive. I told myself to get over trying to be too holy. I thought, what's wrong with a kiss?

During the next few months, Paul and I spent a lot of time together. It was a new year, 1968, and my eighteenth birthday was near. On my birthday, February 17, 1968, Paul took me out to dinner at the Dublin House in downtown Seattle. Piano music was playing in the background and the ambiance was romantic. It was a beautiful restaurant with décor that made me feel like I was on a romantic island.

During dessert, Paul passed me a beautifully wrapped little box. I opened it and there was a ring.

"Will you marry me?" Paul asked.

My heart was racing but I gathered myself.

"Yes!" I said. He placed the ring on my finger and gave me a quick kiss. I was elated to be engaged to this man. It was a dream that had come true.

Paul asked me to pick a date for the wedding. I knew it had to be the seventeenth day since I was born on the seventeenth of February. So I chose August 17, 1968. I felt like I was floating high above the clouds, like a queen. But I was also anxious about the unexpected. When we got back to my house, I didn't tell my mom right away because I was still in high school and I felt she would not be okay with me getting married so young.

Paul wanted me to move in with him, but I said no. Shacking up with him before marriage was not okay. Paul respected me for my decision. However, we did have unplanned sex, only once. It was my first encounter with sex and I became pregnant. So there I was getting ready to graduate high school, experiencing nausea daily from the pregnancy, and planning our wedding. I thought my sickness was punishment from God for not waiting until marriage, but later came to understand God's Grace and Mercy are always available.

We were married on August 17, 1968, and I was four months' pregnant. My first child,

Paul, Jr., was born two weeks early on December 29, 1968. Soon my second child, Shawn Marie Davis, was born on October 18, 1970. After our second child, Paul and I decided I would start taking birth control pills. But the pills failed us and on September 25, 1972, Tara Ann Davis was born.

Chapter 3

MARRIED LIFE

"Therefore, what God has joined together, let no one separate."

(Mark 10:9)

At twenty-three years old, I was diagnosed with chronic high blood pressure and my physician expressed concern about me having additional children because it could put me at risk for stroke and the baby could be born deformed. I did become pregnant two additional times, but these pregnancies were terminated early with a DNC procedure. I wasn't okay with this process and didn't want to repeat it, so Paul and I decided I would have tubal ligation surgery. I was admitted to the hospital in the fall of 1974 and had the tubal removal of at least half of my tubes. I was assured that this process was ninety-nine percent guaranteed to prevent pregnancy.

However, one year later, in 1975, I became pregnant. My sixth pregnancy. I firmly told my doctor, Dr. B. Donaldson, that I was going to keep this baby and wasn't worried about having a stroke during labor, nor was I concerned about the baby potentially being deformed.

I prayed about keeping this baby and my faith in God and belief in His Word comforted me. I strongly believed all would go well. And it did! A healthy baby boy, Andre Deon Davis, was born October 29, 1976. I was so thankful and grateful to God. My faith was becoming stronger. God had brought me through and defied what my doctor had said to me. I didn't want fear to drive my decisions.

My walk with Jesus Christ carried me through the mental, physical, and emotional pain of growing up in a single-parent household with a mother whose health was challenged with chronic high blood pressure. I never knew if my mom would be around to see me grow up and that provoked a great deal of anxiety in me. To help me calm my anxious thoughts, I memorized several scriptures to call upon at my time of need, such as Psalm 23 and Psalm 121.

I believed that God would not put more on me than I could bear. God was always faithful to what His Word said. This was tested when my mom had a stroke on November 11, 1973, that took her away for good. I received a call early Sunday morning from my sister Carla, who reported, "I can't wake Mom up!" I was living at 3726 South Cloverdale in south Seattle. I jumped into my car and went over to the house at 3212 East Terrace in the Leschi district.

Upon my arrival, I was informed that the medics were with my mom in her bedroom. The medics had been working on trying to revive her but were unsuccessful. I drew up enough strength from a power greater than myself whom I call God and went to my mom's bedroom, where she was lying on the bed in her undergarments. She looked so peaceful, as if she were sleeping. The reality hit me in the gut. My mother was gone forever. Deceased. I fell to my knees in tears. I tried to scream but nothing came out. No words could describe the helplessness and emotional pain I felt.

There were several people in the house and so much was going on as I sat in shock and numbness. I was twenty-three years old and the go-to person in the family, the one who had to make all funeral plans and get everything together. So I did what was necessary.

I had my faith. I believed that God would walk me through each step and so I trusted him and remained strong. There were times when I was in and out of darkness, fear, grief, and despair. I decided that I could feel scared and still do what I needed to do with God on my side and in my spirit. I didn't have to see the end results to know that God had me covered through all times. There is nothing too big for God. This was another test that further built my faith.

At twenty-six years old, I was married with four children, two sons and two daughters. I was a stay-at-home mom. Miss Betty Crocker Davis. My husband believed that working to make chump change wasn't worth my leaving our home and paying for child care.

He said, "All you need to do is have my dinner ready when I return home, iron my shirts for work, take care our children, and keep the house clean."

So I did. At first, I thought I had a good deal going and felt privileged. I could choose how to spend my day. Shopping. Baking. Cooking. Cleaning.

Paul wouldn't allow me to write checks unless he gave me a single check purposely for groceries; otherwise, I didn't have access to the checkbook. He often treated me like I was a child, not capable of doing things outside the home on my own. I had a curfew when I went out and had to ask permission to use our 1968 Pontiac GTO.

One time when I was out too long with the car, I was met with a slap in the face and a scolding as I walked in the door. On another occasion, my sister Carla was with me. We had been visiting our mother's grave and I had taken the car without his permission. When we returned home, I was slapped and grabbed with both hands and told not to take the car without his permission. My sister Carla was ready to fight Paul, so he backed off. Another time I came home and was met with a slap in front of my kids. After this, I was ready to leave the marriage. I stopped caring about him and felt the need to take care of myself. I prayed. "Those who wait on the Lord shall renew their strength, they shall mount up on wings like eagles, they shall run and not become weary and walk and not faint." (Isaiah 40:31)

In my heart I didn't believe Paul was a violent man. I believed he was just stressed from his job at the Boeing Company and took out his frustration on me. I knew that having another car would allow me more freedom to venture out. My mother-in-law surprised me and gave me her old, beat-up car, a red-and-white Rambler. I was so happy to have my own transportation, which gave me more independence. I used to think that being a stay-at-home housewife was a gift, but then I realized it was a gift that came with a price: control and dependence on my husband. It wasn't long before the 1968 Pontiac GTO broke down and Paul purchased a used Ford Granada.

Chapter 4

GOD SUSTAINS ME

"Don't be afraid, for I am with you. Don't be discouraged, for I am your God. I will strengthen you and help you. I will hold you up with my victorious right hand."

(Isaiah 41:10)

In 1981, I worked briefly for the Boeing Company in Kent, then moved to 14th Avenue South to work at Plant II in Radiation Health Protection. During this time, we began our participation in an annual Boeing canoe trip down the Skagit River for employees and their families. The first year that Paul and I went, this adventure was a little scary, but fun. The following year, I asked my brother and his wife, neighbors, and friends to come along with us. My brother Michael was hesitant, but he trusted Paul and me. Some of us piled in our neighbor's van and others drove. We caravanned to Concrete, Washington. I glanced out the car window and noticed that the Skagit River was moving faster than I recalled last year. My heart began pounding and I began having second thoughts about the trip.

Once we arrived, we made our way to board the excursion bus that would take us to where we would board the canoe (two people per canoe). We were given instructions on how to paddle down the Skagit River back to where our cars were parked.

It was approximately a twenty-five-mile trip down the river back to our vehicles. We were given further instructions about how to use paddles when moving through rapids on the river. We were told to keep our life jackets on and to keep away from the embankment as trees and branches hung over the water's edge, making it difficult to paddle through. There were two people in each canoe, so my brother Michael shared a canoe with his wife, Lucille. Lucille was a tiny woman but strong mentally and wasn't scared of much. She encouraged Michael to board the canoe and try to relax.

As we boarded the canoes, my brother Michael became afraid. The river was flowing too fast and he was getting dizzy. Michael stood up as he hollered for Paul's help to get out of the canoe. I was praying and asking God to calm both my brother and me. My heart felt like it was going to explode. I was afraid for my brother and I wanted to prevent myself from having a panic attack. We finally came to a place in the river where we could pull over to shore and get out of the canoe. Everyone stopped, so we decided to take this time to eat the sack lunches that we brought with us. We ate and talked about the madness of how fast the river was moving. My brother said he was not getting back in the canoe.

The challenge was that his wife needed a partner in order to continue down the river to get back to our vehicles. So I decided to abandon the trip and join my brother. We hiked through the woods in hopes of getting to the other side of the riverbank so we could walk back to our cars. When we reached a clearing, we saw that there was another river between us, so we hiked back to the canoes. Our only option was to get back in the canoes and continue down the river. I climbed into the canoe, my heart pounding. I sat in front, and Paul was in the back, navigating the canoe with me. As soon as we pushed off into the river, an overwhelming feeling of anxiety and fear came over me. Our canoe was heading too close to the embankment and tree branches were hanging above our heads. We were in the bend of the river. I felt a panic attack coming on and told Paul that we were too close to the trees.

"Paddle fast!" I yelled, hoping Paul could avoid hitting the tree branches.

"Relax, woman. We are fine," Paul said.

A tree branch hit me in the back of the head, knocking me into the water. The canoe tipped over and the cross-current tossed me around underwater. I was in and out of consciousness. I was drowning.

I prayed to God to please help me. I thought, "I'm not going to see my children again. How will they cope with my death?"

I felt God's peace wash over me. Even in my struggle, every time I was conscious, I felt God's presence and comfort.

"Please stop fighting or we're both going to drown," said Paul.

"Okay," I said, as consciousness left me.

I awoke to the sound of a motorboat beside my floating body and was pulled into the boat.

My body felt heavy with all my wet clothing, but I felt calm, at peace.

I thanked God for saving me. I knew that He sent that boat down the Skagit River to pick me up. To this day, I still have no idea who was driving that boat, which took me to shore.

When I arrived at the shore, I was removed from the boat and placed on top of several blankets on the ground. I was in shock. I was surrounded by both people I knew and strangers. I was placed in the ambulance and taken to Sedro-Wooley Hospital, where it was determined my lungs were clear, but the hospital kept me briefly for observation. Words can't fully express my emotions and thankfulness for living through this experience and having the opportunity to see my children again. This has taught me to never take a moment for granted.

My friend Steve, who was also on the trip, picked me up from the hospital and took me back to where our cars were parked. My family and friends were there waiting. Everyone was there … except Paul.

"Where's Paul?" I asked.

I heard someone say, "They're still searching for him."

It was getting dark so I was informed that the search would continue the next day.

I panicked.

How was I going to return home without Paul? What would I tell our children about their father? Andre was four years old, Tara was eight, Shawn was ten, and Paul Jr. was twelve.

Some of our family members walked with me through the door of our house at 3726 South Cloverdale. I was red-eyed from crying and still fighting back tears. My hair and clothes were a mess.

"What happened? Where's Dad?"

How could I answer? I could hear someone explain to them that their dad was missing and that the search team would resume the search tomorrow. They reassured my children, "Your dad is a good swimmer and probably got out of the water and is just lost right now."

My kids cried and asked a million questions, but I was too exhausted to answer. I went to my bedroom and fell across the bed and slept. Early the next morning I called to ask when the search would continue for my husband. I was informed that divers were already out and sweeping the river for him and that they would call me when they had an update.

The accident took place June 27, 1981, around three o'clock in the afternoon. Two weeks later, on a Sunday morning, I got the call.

The Skagit County coroner said they found Paul's body, which was in same place we tipped over in the river, and that his body was caught up in debris. I was asked to send someone to identify Paul's body as it would be too traumatic for me. Paul's brother Isaac went to identify him and returned some of his belongings to me. A charm Paul had around his neck, his driver's license, a watch, and some change in his pocket—all of which I still have today.

I was numb. Because I never saw Paul's body, part of me believed he could've gotten out of the water and was still alive, had amnesia, and could walk through the door at any moment. My kids believed the same off and on for years. It's difficult to bring closure to the loss of a loved one when you don't see the body to confirm the death.

My children and I became inseparable. We distracted ourselves with church activities and movie marathon nights. We did everything together. There were nights when we all camped out in my bedroom. The boys slept in their sleeping bags on the floor at the foot of my bed and my youngest daughter slept in her sleeping bag on the other side of bed. My oldest daughter slept in bed with me because she was a quiet sleeper, moved very little, and didn't kick me while sleeping.

We went to family counseling for a short time and were encouraged to call on our faith in God and our church family and community for support, which we did.

It was my belief in God and my personal walk of faith that brought me through this difficult time, along with daily prayers with family, friends, and my church. I hung reaffirming scriptures in my car and all around the house. "I can do all things through Christ who strengthens me." "Cast all your cares on Him because He cares for you." These scriptures helped me move through each day. God was lifting me, directing me, and sending people into my life to comfort me at just the right time. I immersed myself in my faith and my children were right by my side. I was in the choir and found singing to be therapeutic, so I sang often.

There were times when my children and I sang together and visited other churches and sang praises. The one song my adult children still remember is "I Want Jesus to Walk with Me." Even today we sing it with delight and praise.

During this time, there were many wonderful people around me. And even though there were a few men who tried to take advantage of my grief, God was watching out for me.

I dated several men from all cultures and professions—grocery store clerks, attorneys, doctors, policemen, musicians, and performing artists. One was a stage actor from New York. Ron and I came close to a commitment until he shared with me that he had two small children and was estranged from their mom.

I extended an invitation for dinner to a man named John, whom I'd known for a while. He was a musician. During dinner with all four of my children around the table, my youngest son Andre blurted out, "My mom has scoliosis." We all busted into laughter. Andre was protective and wanted to run this man away, and I was fine with that.

I met many men who wanted to take care of me and my children, but I was always suspicious about their motives. I had lots of male attention and felt there was often a hidden agenda. I didn't trust easy and had to protect my children from perverts.

There were good days and challenging days. Over time, I began having more good days and started looking for employment. I got a part-time job at the University of Washington. It was nice to ease into working again. I often dealt with panic attacks, which limited my activities and the amount of time I could be away from home.

Dating as a single parent was different. Most men ran when I told them I had four children. I think these goofballs were thinking I was looking for someone to help raise my children. Not.

I decided to remain single until my children were out of school. In 1989, while working at the University of Washington and preparing to leave the physician assistant program, I applied for a position at the Veterans Administration Medical Center. I was excited to learn something different and experience a new environment. Being employed at the University of Washington in an academic environment prompted my desire to complete my undergrad and graduate degrees.

Chapter 5

GOD GIVES BEAUTY FOR ASHES

"God gives beauty for ashes, joy for mourning, and praise for despair."

(Isaiah 61:3)

While working temporarily at the VA, in the fall of 1990, I met Nathaniel Roberts (his friends called him Robbie) in the hallway. He was well-dressed, had a great smile, and smelled good. Soon we were having lunch on a daily basis. During our second lunch date he disclosed that his wife passed away in 1983 and I shared that my spouse passed in 1981. We talked about how painful the loss was for both of us and agreed that we would never marry again. Robbie and I continued to see each other and dated throughout the years, even after I returned to work at the University of Washington, Office of Minority Affairs, Early Scholars Outreach Program (ESOP).

Our first real date was on April 10, 1991. Robbie asked me to dinner at Red Lobster in Federal Way, Washington, and to see a movie after dinner, "The Five Heartbeats." We had a lovely time. We held hands during the movie, and I felt at home in my heart with Robbie. After the movie, Robbie dropped me off at the park-and-ride in Midway and headed home to Tacoma.

I walked through the door at home and the telephone was ringing.

"James died." It was my sister's voice on the other end of the line.

I felt alone. I was numb. How? How did our brother die? My heart sank.

"What happened? Was he by himself?" I said.

My sister told me that he accidentally overdosed. James was a kind and loving soul who got caught up in an ugly heroin habit. Five years earlier he had been shot. He claimed that the pain medication never adequately addressed his pain so he injected heroin.

Robbie and I continued to date and in May 1995, he asked me to be his lady, but I said "No." We were great friends and I didn't want to ruin our friendship. Robbie never gave up on me and asked me again on his birthday, July 27, 1995. I decided I would give it serious thought. By December 1995 I was ready to give our relationship a chance, so I finally said "Yes."

I completed undergrad and graduate school in June 1997. My children were all out of school and my youngest son was getting ready for college, but he had a few blessings that slowed his process ... like a beautiful daughter, Ashane Davis. A few years later, my handsome grandson came along, Andre Davis, Jr. In the meantime, my oldest son Paul had two sons, Asante and Elijah Davis; my daughter Shawn had one son, Jayden; and my youngest daughter Tara Davis had three sons, Lake, Loren and Kai.

I was blessed to have all these wonderful grandkids! My grown children and I continued to be close and when I began to plan my marriage to Robbie, August 23, 1997, all my grown children were in the wedding.

Prior to getting married, I wanted to take a trip to UC Berkeley, California, to have Robbie meet my dad and ask for my hand in marriage. We took the Coast Starlight train to meet up with my dad for a few days. Robbie asked my dad for permission to marry me and, of course, my dad smiled and said, "That's fine with me." My dad was a quiet, soft-spoken man who had stopped drinking years ago, but not before some physical and mental damage had occurred. My dad was dealing with the beginning stages of Alzheimer's Disease in 1997; however, we didn't find out how severe his symptoms were until a few years later. My dad was always a sweet man, even when he was intoxicated. I wrote a long letter to my dad, thanking him for giving me life despite the fact he wasn't always around. I thanked my dad for doing the best he could with what he had and stopped being angry at him for not showing up in my life sooner. In the Word of God, it speaks to forgiving others for their trespasses so God can forgive us for our trespasses. I had so much peace in my heart after writing that letter of love, thankfulness, and forgiveness.

Upon our return from Berkeley, California, we continued to plan our wedding. My oldest son Paul wrote a song called "A Friend," a beautiful song that was so fitting for my wedding. Paul played most of the music during our wedding except for the Lord's Prayer, which was played by my dear friend, Dr. Carlene Brown, and the song of entry, "You and I" sung by Vanessa Love. Robbie and I had a fantastic wedding—the processional took fifteen minutes by itself. We had over thirty folks in our wedding party and both of my sons walked me in. It was a lovely affair.

Robbie and I purchased our home in Lynnwood, Washington. We were the first occupants of this house.

We loved on each other and we were living our lives in blessed peace, joy, and happiness. Robbie retired from the Veterans Administration the same year we married and brought me an application for employment as an Addiction Therapist. In April 1998, I was employed at the VA in the Mental Health Department, Addictions Treatment Center. I truly enjoyed my career, spent working with the veterans at the VA. Robbie was a veteran also. He served twenty years in the Air Force prior to his military retirement and received good benefits, which would come in handy as Robbie was diagnosed with dementia in May 2003 and later, Alzheimer's Disease, in June 2007.

Having great benefits was a tremendous help for me due to Robbie's care needs, such as getting him in the shower, dressing him, preparing Medisets, managing his blood sugar, etc. This worked out well until Robbie's care needs became greater than I could manage while working full time, so I had to take an early retirement in November 2009 to take care of him around the clock. Nothing could prepare me for the daily care that Robbie required. There were days when Robbie did well, he was not argumentative, and I learned early to not argue with him anyway because it was pointless. Then there were days when Robbie appeared lucid and I didn't see any signs of dementia. Those days became further and further apart until they became rare. We were often in the emergency room in the middle of the night due to Robbie's blood sugar dropping so low that he became unresponsive. During those critical times, I was on the telephone with nursing services, getting guidance on how to increase Robbie's blood sugar. Robbie had several falls and I wasn't able to get him up, so again, the 911 calls were piling up. The Fire Department and

Medic One urged me to consider placing my husband in assisted living because of all the 911 calls and reported falls. I was warned to take another approach.

My role as a wife was being challenged by my role as my husband's caregiver. Witnessing this loving, bright, intelligent man be taken down slowly by the disease of Alzheimer's was a long, heart-wrenching journey. Robbie was a gunner in the Air Force, where he was exposed to Agent Orange, became service-connected for diabetes, high blood pressure, PTSD, prostate cancer, and the list goes on. Robbie was a one hundred percent service-connected veteran, which allowed benefits for his personal care, including placement in VA long-term care. I became his representative payee as he was deemed incompetent to manage his affairs and funds from the VA due his diagnosis of Alzheimer's Disease dementia.

The signs of dementia were subtle at first: forgetting where he put his keys, wallet, and checkbook; leaving keys in the door; forgetting to turn water off; not knowing the difference between the remote and the telephone; identifying the difference between the doorbell or telephone ringing; or knowing the day of the week. There were some mornings when Robbie would wake up and say, "I am ready to go home." I thought he meant home to the Lord, so I would graciously say, "Honey, you are home, can I help you? What do you need? I got you."

Robbie was employed at H&R Block part time after retiring from the Seattle VA in 1997. He was doing well there until he wasn't. He began to forget information needed to file income taxes and was let go in 2003. Little by little, Robbie lost his independence. One of the hardest things was when his driver's license was taken away. He was informed that due to being diagnosed with dementia, he would have to retake the written and driver's exams. He took the written test and was allowed to take it five times before he passed it. The first time out for his driver's test, Robbie failed it and gave me his keys. I could feel his heartache and his dignity being stripped. I tried with everything I had to encourage him by reminding him of what a fine man of integrity he was and had always been. I constantly told him how much I loved him and how I "had his back" and would never leave him. The reassurance was needed daily. Robbie was fifteen years older than I and he thought I was going to go out and get a younger man. He didn't understand how much I loved him and would be there until death did us part.

The journey continued downhill. Robbie had multiple health issues that kept us in the doctor's office, signs of a heart attack, and brittle diabetes, which made it difficult to manage his blood sugar. It dropped in the middle of the night to 40 and I was often calling 911, giving Robbie honey to bring up his blood sugar and some protein to stabilize him. Robbie often was up during the night to pee. He would miss the toilet and end up on the bathroom floor, partially unconscious.

Robbie was incontinent and I often would change his clothes and the linens in the middle of the night. He wore men's Depends, but they often leaked. I had all the supplies necessary for the home, shower buddy, elevator chair lift, toilet seat lifts, bars, padding, etc. My day would consist of getting Robbie up and in the shower, dressed, placing him in the elevator chair lift that the VA had installed in our home, and transporting him downstairs, where I would test his blood sugar levels, give him insulin, make him breakfast, and administer his many medications. I made up Medisets to last for 6 weeks. Robbie had a bag of medications to take and I had to keep track of them all. I became his nurse and worked around the clock, doing what I felt was needed. Several folks, including my family, social workers, my church family, and my doctor, encouraged me to look into respite care for Robbie because I was sleep-deprived but didn't know it. I was doing what I knew to do; after all, he was my husband. After verbally exploding one day at Robbie, I knew it was time for something to change, so I looked into respite care for a week. He first went to the Seattle VA, but he was left unsupervised and wandered off.

In May of 2011, I was informed that the American Lake VA in Tacoma, Washington, had a locked dementia unit where Robbie would be safe. Robbie and I resided in Lynnwood, Washington. I tried respite care for Robbie, reluctantly, for a week. I was amazed at how much better and more rested I felt, but I still missed Robbie, so I was happy to pick him up and take him home.

Once he was home, he continued to decline and became more difficult to manage. I had a caregiver, Lawrence, who was in our home for four hours a day, but Robbie would tell him, "My wife will do it. She can help me." He refused to let the care provider help out.

Eventually, Lawrence began to bond with Robbie and was allowed to help with toileting and to assist with Robbie's showers on some days. Lawrence would sit with Robbie and watch court TV shows and The Price is Right. When Robbie fell asleep, Lawrence would clean the kitchen, vacuum, sweep, and do Robbie's laundry.

Robbie continued to decline, and I became concerned about his safety. I became borderline suicidal and wasn't taking care of myself. I didn't realize how poor my health was becoming.

I talked with a friend in social work, who expressed concern and said she planned to make a call to see how soon Robbie could be admitted for long-term inpatient care at the American Lake Dementia Unit. The next day, a dear friend, Taylene, called me with a bed in the unit for Robbie.

After his birthday celebration on July 27, 2011, I began to pack up some clothes and toiletries for him to be admitted to the dementia unit. I couldn't hold back the tears. I cried as I packed his clothes and kept telling myself, "It's for Robbie's safety. It has to be this way." On July 29, 2011, with Robbie's suitcase ready for the trip, I asked Lawrence to ride with us and we headed out to American Lake.

I talked to Robbie on the way, telling him that he would need to stay in the hospital for a while. He asked me how long and I told him I didn't know, but in my gut, I knew he wouldn't be coming home. Ever.

The check-in process seemed to take forever. My heart was pounding the entire time. Robbie asked me questions about his stay there. The intake nurse was kind and answered Robbie's questions. Robbie had a private room, which was set up nicely. His room overlooked the garden. It was a beautiful facility, but nothing could take away the inner pain I felt. When it was time to say goodbye to Robbie, I fought hard to hold back the tears and told him I would see him later. I cried off and on all the way back to Lynnwood as Lawrence tried to comfort me. I didn't sleep the first few nights. I was extremely lonely, depressed, and full of grief. The staff suggested that I give Robbie a few weeks to adjust to the unit before I returned for a visit. I waited almost two weeks, but I called daily.

When I finally visited, he was happy to see me. We held on to each other and we both cried. Robbie said, "I thought we would always be together."

"Yes, honey, we will be together. I'm here with you and will always come and be here with you," I said. We held each other for a long time.

I talked to Robbie daily and visited him often. We said our prayers together nightly (Lord's Prayer) and as Robbie's vocabulary became limited, he would repeat the Lord's Prayer after me the best he could.

He didn't have a sense of time and place. Sometimes I would visit with him half the day and when I would return home, a staff person would put Robbie on the telephone. "How come you haven't been to see me?" he would ask.

I wouldn't argue with him. "Honey, I was there earlier and will see you later." He seemed to be happy with that. My heart screamed with sorrow. I missed Robbie every day and night, no matter how much time passed, and my heart and soul cried out. Nights were extremely hard and reminded me of the sweet ritual Robbie and I had when preparing for bed. We would listen to soft music and I would rub lotion on him and sometimes a cream on his knees for aches. We would cuddle and say our prayers. It was a precious time of love, grace, and thankfulness for the day and each other.

Unshakeable Faith

Chapter 6

THY WILL BE DONE

"I can do nothing on my own. As I hear, I judge, and my judgment is just, because I seek not my own will but the will of him who sent me."

(John 5:30)

On February 7, 2012, I was a guest of Dave Isay on New Day Northwest to talk about my journey as Robbie's caregiver. Dave selected my interview with StoryCorps from October 2008 for the hour taping. My story is filed in the Library of Congress. StoryCorps allows you to leave messages about your loved ones, preserve experiences about their lives, and have future family members listen and appreciate your loved ones who have passed on. It was therapeutic sharing with StoryCorps. I was especially touched to have my personal story selected out of thousands of stories for Dave Isay's book, All There Is: Love Stories from StoryCorps.

I visited Robbie four times a week, staying half the day and sometimes into the evening. The staff would say, "Mrs. Roberts, you need to go home and take care of yourself." It was just too difficult to leave Robbie. As time went on, though, I began to cut back my visiting hours. When Robbie was no longer able to feed himself, I fed him. I enjoyed taking care of him, but it was sad to see him continue to decline. Robbie and I had wonderful visits. I would give him haircuts, rub lotion on him, sing to him, and we would hold hands. Sometimes I would break into a song and he would laugh. We went for walks in the facility and outside. The grounds were beautiful, surrounded by a lake. Robbie loved being outside. When Robbie's mobility became challenged, I would push him in his wheelchair.

On our fifteenth wedding anniversary, August 23, 2012, the second year that Robbie was in the facility, a friend of mine came down to play keyboards for us. I also started taking care of myself, doing things for me. I auditioned for the musical, Black Nativity and performed in twenty-six shows, Tuesday through Sunday, so I visited Robbie on Mondays for those two months.

I had quarterly meetings with the disciplinary team regarding Robbie's health status. Robbie didn't want to be resuscitated or kept alive on machines. Every time the telephone rang, my heart would skip a beat and I would pray this wasn't the final call telling me Robbie was gone.

I took every advantage of loving on him. I told him how much I loved him and that I was there for him always. He would smile and with his limited vocabulary, say, "That's good. That's nice. I love you." He would kiss my hands and reach out to me when he saw me coming down the hall. Often, he was waiting at the door for me when I was buzzed in.

Eventually, Robbie couldn't do anything on his own. There was a lift to get him out of bed into his wheelchair or into the shower. He hated taking showers and I asked staff members to be gentle with him. Most staff in the dementia unit were fantastic and were kind and loving to Robbie. There were a few who hurried Robbie, which bothered him, and he would say, "Wait a minute."

Robbie's vocabulary became extremely limited. He also repeated the same word over and over again, which caused the staff to isolate him from the other patients. The word he kept repeating was "Hello." How lovely is that?

One evening in September 2014, I received a call that Robbie was nonresponsive and was on the way to Madigan Army Medical Center. I called my daughter, who rode to the hospital with me.

We were escorted to where Robbie lay unresponsive with an extremely slow heart rate.

"Hi, honey. I'm here. Please open your eyes," I said.

Robbie opened his eyes, squeezed my hand, and looked at me with contentment. I assured him that I would be there for him and do everything in my power to make sure he received the treatment he needed.

I signed the required documents to move forward with Robbie's treatment, which included inserting a line in his neck to distribute the medication he needed to stabilize him. The medical care team assured me they would be gentle with him, so I agreed.

I stayed in the intensive care unit with Robbie the entire week he was there. A nice couple from our church, Pat and Donald Fleeks, came up to sit with Robbie, too. I was scared that Robbie wouldn't come out of this trauma. He had a severe infection in his stomach and bowels. But after a week, Robbie was returned to American Lake. He was still very weak. I kept his family informed and they would visit sometimes. Some of Robbie's family were angry with me for placing him in a nursing facility and wanted me to continue taking care of him at home. I felt guilty about this and held on to this guilt until I realized their thinking was unrealistic. I was the one on this journey and it was ripping me apart.

I didn't care for freeway driving, yet I drove several times a week in all kinds of weather to visit my husband, whom I loved very much. My love for Robbie motivated me to get on the freeway despite my anxiety and drive to American Lake. I prayed daily and had a special tape I listened to on the road. An instrumental tape of gospel music, easy, soft and soothing music that I was given from Shannon, my massage therapist. I played this music from August 2011 to December 2014.

December 4, 2014, was my final visit with Robbie. I didn't know it at the time, but in my gut I felt this visit was different. Robbie was sleepy. I loved on him and hugged him goodbye before heading down the hall to attend the caregiver support group.

Pat and Donald Fleeks came to visit Robbie while I was at the group. During the group meeting I shared my thoughts about not wanting to make a decision to keep Robbie alive should he end up back in the emergency room. I prayed for God's will to be done and to let go of my will to keep Robbie around if he was ready to go. Robbie was a proud man of dignity and I knew he didn't care for his new normal, especially not being able to do anything for himself. I could see it in his eyes.

After the meeting I returned to hug and kiss Robbie goodbye. He was in and out of sleep. I told him I loved him and would see him on Saturday.

On Saturday, around four o'clock in the afternoon, I received a telephone call that Robbie had passed away in his sleep. I held the telephone in silence, knowing the final call was here.

I said, "What happened?"

The staff said that Robbie was fed a good lunch. He smiled as Alice was feeding him and when a staff member went to wake him for dinner, he had already passed away in his sleep.

I was numb. I was asked if I wanted to come down and say goodbye to Robbie before they removed his body. I said no. In my spirit and mind, Robbie was already gone. I chose to remember Robbie's smile and face when I last saw him on Thursday, December 4, 2014.

I called each of my kids and close family members, who all came over and spent the evening with me. I cried off and on the entire evening. I had mixed emotions. I knew Robbie was ready to go home to the Lord, so how could I be too sad? But I couldn't get my heart and mind to line up.

Unshakeable Faith

Chapter 7

GOD DIRECTS MY PATH

"Let the morning bring me word of your unfailing love, for I have put my trust in you. Show me the way I should go, for to you I entrust my life."

(Psalm 143:8)

There was much planning to do. I would have to move because when a veteran passes away, his funds are taken away also. I wasn't sure where I was going to move but focused on funeral arrangements, which all fell into place nicely. Robbie's family said they would like to see him even though I hadn't planned for a viewing. I made adjustments and there was a viewing a day before the funeral service. I had to be there, but I wouldn't look at Robbie's deceased body. His family sat in the room with him for over an hour and afterwards I left Marlatt Funeral Home. I was so pleased to be away from there.

The funeral service went well, as family and friends spoke highly of my dear husband Robbie. I asked Josie Howell to sing. Robbie loved her voice. It was a beautiful celebration of life and during the burial service at Tahoma National Cemetery, a large rainbow covered us. The staff there said they had never seen this before.

With the funeral behind me, it was time to move. Several months prior to Robbie's passing, I had run into an old buddy from childhood, Stan, who had taken me down to see Robbie several times and was aware of my need to move. He offered me a place below where he stayed in Lakeridge. The timing was perfect, so

I took him up on his offer and he helped me move.

He had a seven-bedroom home and downstairs was equipped with a kitchen, living room, and two plus bedrooms. I had the nerve to be picky about my bedroom being downstairs, so Stan cleared out one of the upstairs bedrooms. I was in a home with a beautiful, sweeping view of Lake Washington and windows that crossed the entire living and dining room. I woke up to God's creation and was so pleased to share this home with Stan, who also helped me with lots of government paperwork. It was truly a blessing for me, and I was grateful to Stan.

I believe that God places people in our paths for his glory and it was not a coincidence. God giveth and he taketh away. God has never left me throughout my life journey, and I was able to move through my grief knowing I had a real friend in Stan. He would say, "I will take a bullet for you." That's a real friend, although I hoped he would never have to take a bullet for me. Stan knew my family from the 1960s. He also knew my first husband Paul, and he knew of Robbie. Stan was in and out of my life for over fifty years and continues to be my friend today.

Stan claimed he was not a man who could be married, which worked for both of us, because we would have killed each other. We were both spoiled and used to having things our own way. Neither one of us gives in. We are old school that way. However, Stan has been my guardian angel. I appreciate his friendship. We enjoy each other's company because we've known each other for decades and know each other well.

One day in June 2017, I met a nice man from Alaska named Ronald. He was attending my church with his daughter, whom I knew from Connections Bible study. During the Connections group many of our members—including me—would talk about a desire to meet a nice companion. Beatrice, one of the women in the group, said she would like me to meet her dad, Ronald.

Ronald gave me a holy hug and we have been talking, interacting, and dating ever since. He is a quiet man, but when he speaks, his words are powerful. He travels with his family, going on camping trips and traveling to other exciting places. I am not big on camping or traveling, but I'm willing to consider it.

Ronald returned to Alaska in March 2018 to move some things out of his condo and was contemplating selling his place because we were sharing a life together now. He asked me to marry him on July 19, 2018, and we were married on December 15, 2018.

Unshakeable Faith

Chapter 8

GOD IS ALWAYS WITH ME

"Be strong and courageous. Do not be afraid; do not be discouraged, for the LORD your God is with you wherever you go."

(Joshua 1:9)

As I look back on all the adversities—my brother's death and the impact on my mother from losing her firstborn son; losing my beautiful and vibrant mom at the young age of fifty; the tragedy of my first husband's death and the guilt I felt for many years about raising our children without their father—I know God was always there with me, throughout it all. He gifted me with another marriage and a beautiful experience as a caregiver. God carried both Robbie and me through this heart-wrenching time and Robbie, even in his diminishing state, never forgot who I was.

My faith in God gave me courage to move forward with hope in my heart and live in the possibility of endless blessings. He turned my sorrow into joy, love, and laughter again.

Knowing that God has carried me through every tragedy in my life and will continue to be there every step of the way, through whatever future trials and tribulations I may face, gives me comfort and strengthens my faith.

God has proven to me over and over again that the saying, "With God all things are possible" is undeniably true. I trust Him with everything in my life!

No matter what difficulties I have faced, God has always shown me a way out by placing certain people strategically in my path who have supported me and my children. I have learned to listen more, sit in blessed quietness, and wait for God's direction—and to not lean on my own understanding, which can be misguided. My journey is built on faith. I've learned how to be comfortable with not knowing the outcome of my choices and trust that God will reveal my next move in due season and time. As God says in His Word, His thoughts and ways are much higher than ours.

Life is full of the unexpected and I have a choice as to who, what, when, where, and how I bring others into my personal space.

"In all thy ways acknowledge the Lord and He will direct my path." (Prov. 3:5)

Life is full of adversity. Learning how others have persevered can open doors for your own personal growth and provide guidance for managing your own unexpected tragedies.

Know that God is always with you even when you don't feel it or believe it. God is still there and will bring you from valley experiences to mountain-top victories. God has replaced my losses with everything from extended brothers/sisters to virtuous women mentors, has sustained my health, has addressed my fear about being raped during a career spent working with thousands of male veterans, fear-free. He has given me several close friends and a new best friend to fill the void of Terry, whom I loved dearly. And now, He's given me a God-fearing husband with whom I'm sharing a life of love, commitment, favor of God, and our families have blended remarkably well.

My life is more enhanced with God's love. Today I enjoy more joy, laughter, and peace of mind than I could've ever imagined. I'm surrounded by God's love and creation daily and I long to seek to know God more.

So when trials and tribulations come along, cling to God's unchanging hand because you never know what miracles are near if you hold on and never give up. Walk through the pain believing brighter days and loving moments are in view.

"For the Lord your God is a merciful God.
He will not leave you or destroy you."
(Deut. 4:31)

APPENDIX

God awakened me one morning with thoughts of blessings and questions regarding how my life might look if I had not experienced multiple losses and traumas. God's answer to my questions was the inspiration for this book.

SUMMARY OF SIGNIFICANT EVENTS

Age 4: Dad left home and my life.

Age 10: Oldest brother Simmie died by drowning.

Age 23: My mother died at age 50 due to poor health (HBP) and anxiety and suffered years of physical and mental abuse from men prior to her death.

Age 24: Raped by a friend of Paul's in our home while my children played out back.

Age 31: My first husband Paul died tragically leaving me with 4 children to raise.

Age 41: My brother James' overdosed and died at age 42.

Age 50-68: Eleven surgeries and poor health due to chronic High Blood Pressure/Anxiety Disorder.

Age 51: Breast cancer survivor.

Age 64: My second husband died after long journey with Alzheimer's Disease.

Age 65: My best friend Terry died. My brother Robert died later that year in December in nursing facility and I was not informed of his death until a week later. Then my sister Carla died in January of 2016, three weeks later.

WHO'S WHO,
BRIEF BACKGROUND,
AND CURRENT STATUS

*(On top, hand painted picture
mentioned in story)*

Paul Davis Sr.

Born September 4, 1946, Paul was a quiet
man, a deep thinker who loved people.

Drafted into the military at 18 years old and served on a tour of Vietnam that changed his life forever. His nightmares were horrible. He often spent time alone. He enjoyed the gift of gab and we would talk for hours late at night and into the morning. He enjoyed spending time with his children and was out at every track practice and track event when they began athletic activities. He enjoyed the outdoors, swimming and boating, playing cards, dominos and was an easy-going spirit. He enjoyed the simple things in life like watching the TV shows, "Star Trek," "Bewitched," and scary movies, while drinking a "big mouth" Mickey's beer. His life ended too soon at 34 years old in a tragic canoe accident on June 27, 1981. Paul and I had four children together.

Paul Davis Jr.

Born December 29, 1968 and danced to his own drummer. He graduated from Renton High School, entered the Airforce and was a Military Policeman stationed in Egypt where he taught himself how to play piano. When he returned to the U.S., he began creating music and was a music ministry leader. He created and directed several plays, recorded many CD's, played keyboards with several local and professional entertainers, and continues to teach piano and voice lessons. Paul also has a strong background in computer science and is an excellent computer programmer. He was also a financial planner for several years and worked with investors during the dot com era in 2000.

He currently resides in Texas near Dallas and is married with four children.

Shawn Davis-Gocha

Born October 18, 1970 and created her space in a male dominated field—engineering. Graduated from Rainier Beach High School, then graduated from Western Washington with a Bachelor of Science in Electrical Engineering Technology and is currently working at King County Waste Water Engineering as an Instrumentation and Controls Engineer. Shawn also had a 4-year athletic scholarship to play basketball and at United States International University, Sam Houston State University and her final year at Western Washington University.

Shawn was always practical with her money and invested in real estate early, purchasing her first home in her early twenties. She is currently married, with one child.

Tara Davis

Born September 25, 1972, graduated from Rainier Beach High School, attended University of Washington on a 5-year scholarship and graduated with Marketing degree. Played professional basketball overseas, then entered the women's professional league and played first with the Seattle Reign team and then the American Basketball League with Connecticut. Tara returned to graduate school and completed her master's degree in Education and Leadership Policy, emphasizing intercollegiate athletic leadership and is currently the Director of Athletics for Seattle Public Schools. Tara has three boys, the oldest in college at Carnegie Mellon in Pittsburg.

(On the left, resembled his dad, Paul Sr.)

Andre Davis

Born October 29, 1976, Andre was always a self-starter. He graduated from O'Dea High School and completed his undergrad at the University of Washington with a Bachelor of the Arts with a concentration in Sociology. Continued on to graduate school in Marketing/Business and completed his Masters degree. Andre has worked in sales for years and currently works as a real estate agent to supplement his income. Andre is known for his leadership in sales. Andre has two children. His oldest daughter recently graduated from Eastern Washington college and his youngest son graduated from O'Dea High School and plans to attend Arizona State University.

(On right, Robbie's 79ᵗʰ Birthday)

Nathaniel (Robbie) Roberts

Born July 27, 1935 in Memphis Tennessee where he fought the Jim Crow era. He volunteered for the military at 17 years old and served twenty years in the Airforce. Robbie was employed at Seattle Veterans Administration as an accounting supervisor for many years prior to his retirement.

Robbie was a man of integrity, class and kindness. He taught ballroom dancing for fun and wow was he an excellent dancer. Robbie was invited on a cruise with Applegate's ballroom class to teach folks different dances; the swing, rumba, salsa, waltz, etc. Robbie knew all the dances prior to his diagnosis of Alzheimer's Disease.

He had four children prior to our marriage and together we had eight children, all of which were grown prior to our marriage. Robbie passed away December 6, 2014 and is sorely missed. Robbie was what I call a rare man of character, honesty, class and was all about showing who he was, not talking about it.

(On left, Stan in High School)

Stan Brown

My best friend Stan, born in September, graduated Garfield High School in 1968, and attended University of Washington. He started his business TSB Maintenance in 1993 to-present. Stan and I attended Junior High and High School together where he was always my protector, even when I was waiting for Paul to return from Vietnam. Stan has always had my back. He played trumpet and enjoyed music and dance. He loved dressing up and he has enough suits of all colors to last a lifetime, never seeing him in the same suit and shoes twice. Stan and I are still friends today. When you know someone from your childhood who has always been a consistent friend and as Stan says he "would take a bullet for me."

Some people ask why we never married, and the answer is, it just wasn't in the cards for us. Stan was married twice and is currently single.

Ronald Lenear

Born March 25, 1948 in Detroit Michigan. He was drafted into the military and was discharged while in Fairbanks, Alaska where he stayed for over 50 years. He was employed as city worker and retired with good benefits. After retirement he immersed himself into his church and continues to be on fire with his faith and walk with the Lord. Ronald was an active member in his church in Alaska until he was diagnosed with cancer which brought him to Seattle, Washington in January 2017 for treatment at Swedish Hospital. During the end of his year of treatment in Seattle, on June 17, 2017 (Father's Day), we met through his daughter who attends the same bible study group as I did.

We had some rocky times in our relationship as we were getting to know each other, however, these challenges brought us closer together. God knew what he was doing and as Ronald says, "The Lord says when a man finds a woman he finds a good thing."

Ronald proposed to me on July 19, 2018. We were married on December 15, 2018. Ronald is cancer free and full of life. He is a humorous man, easy going, a man of a few words, and enjoys Reggae and Christian music.

He has been retired for several years, and his favorite activities are camping, fishing and traveling to tropical islands which he has done with his family throughout the years.

What I love about Ronald is we pray about everything and have learned to agree to disagree respectfully. Both of us allow the Lord to lead and guide us "not our will but God's will be done."

*(On left, hand painted picture
mentioned in story)*

(Age 24)

Gloria Roberts-Lenear

Gloria is currently enjoying retirement with her husband, family, church family and friends and plans to continue writing as God leads her.

FOUR LETTERS FROM PAUL

First letter dated February 22, 1967

Dear Gloria, I hope this letter finds you in the best of health. As for me, I am still alive. To answer you, there are females here but they're like little girls. To them everything is a game. But let's not discuss the women of a foreign country. They're not that exciting. (smile) I much rather talk about you. I want to know what your likes and dislikes are. What type of things do you like to do? I already know you like bowling. What else makes your life complete?

Oh yes, Jimmy wrote and told me that your club gave a party a few weeks back. Tell me how was it? I was struck when you said that you haven't been to the 4-10 supper club or the House of Entertainment. But tell me, do you like going to cabarets or do you go to them? (smile)

You asked about pictures. Right now, I don't have any, but I had a roll of film I sent to Japan. I should be getting it back pretty soon. When they do come, I will send you one. Until then I would also like a picture of you because I don't have any of you. I can expect a picture in your next letter. This is a sad case. Closing for now.

Love Always, Paul

P.S. Inform the people at home I said hello.

Second letter dated April 20, 1967

Say Doll, what have you been up to since our last correspondence? As for me everything is fine. I hope everything is the same with you. You as of yet haven't told me what you would like from over here. Right now, I am indulging in one of my favorite past times and that is writing you. Of course, it sounds corny, but the truth always does. Say, do you realize I haven't received an answer from my last letter to you. I am beginning to think something is wrong. Oh, I am not getting too personal in your love life filled from day to day, that you can't take a few minutes of your time to write me a few lines. (smile)

You know something, I don't even know your birthday. If it's to come I'd like to send you something and if it's passed I'd also like to send you a delayed one. By the way, mine is September 4th and soon after it I will be home once again. I didn't realize how much I really missed home until I came over to this country. And I'll be glad to leave. All I do is think I'll be home soon and through with the army. It seems that I keep repeating myself about getting out and home. With this thought of leaving I say good bye until our next correspondence.

Love Always, Paul

Third Letter dated June 29, 1967

Dear Gloria, while sitting here yes you guessed it, I am drinking and taking in the sounds. You must think I am an alcoholic. Well I am not, just taking your advice to try and take my mind off my time getting short here. I can't understand why you haven't received my photo as of yet. As soon as I get more you will get some. By the way I have another friend whose name is Arnold who says, and I quote, "if you ever let me get away from you, he won't like it" and he will be there to see you. I say I'd be a fool to let this happen and that is not the liquor talking either. Even though I don't really know you, our letters help me to know more. If I was there, I would know! I want you to carry those pictures with you so I will in a way be with you always. When I come home, I want to see my 8x10 picture sitting in your house.

So have you gone bowling since I left? You do have something on me with ability to ice skate. I have never gone ice skating in my life. I am almost ready to try anything now. After being over here I think anybody would. These pictures you have just sent me, one of them are going downtown and see what these Vietnamese can do in color with them. But I still want one of you in color. By the way that would be a perfect pre-birthday gift. Do you know I will be 21 years old my next birthday?

I believe I have asked you already once, but I will repeat it even though it is personal. What is your hip, waist and bust size? Going to Thailand to shop.

I have been taken off driving duty and put back into the yard. I may be able to make SP/5 that's the same as sergeant. So, I will see what I can do for myself. Everything quiet on the Eastern front. How are things on the Western front? With this, I close until I write again.

Love You, Paul.

P.S. I am mailing a package on June 29, 1967. Like to know how long it takes to get to you.

Fourth Letter written October 30, 1967

Doll, you had complete control over my mind for hours. I am still trying to figure out what I did for those hours. So, I leave your pictures locked up in my locker making sure I don't look at them until it's safe. I don't want to be the cause of several people; including myself getting hurt or killed. I think I have too much to go home to! You, in case you didn't know. I am now looking at the pictures I had hand painted of you. They seemed to have put me in a spell or trance. My mind goes blank and nothing enters my mind but you. Do you know that because of you, I missed one complete run with my truck? When I finally got my senses together again it was about 6pm and all this started at 2pm in the afternoon. But truly, you do have a strange effect on me. As you wonder about me, I also wonder what will really happen when I see you again. Say, I've never seen a girl with a hearing aid and glasses.

That's something else to look forward to isn't it! (smile)

I'd better close now, these folks are running around talking about alert. Take care baby.

Love Always, Paul

Paul returned from Vietnam on November 17, 1967.

QUOTES FROM MY CHILDREN ABOUT THEIR DAD'S PASSING

Paul Davis Jr.: "Just not having guidance and an ear to say this thing here from a man's perspective. I believe I always try to be right and have made the best decisions, but male mentorship has been non-existent. That's the most. The alternate to that is, I'm more courageous because of his selfless example. I will never give up. I know who I am, and kindness is a part of who I am. Great example and that's just as impactful. Mom you have been my rock."

Shawn Davis-Gocha: "I felt the need to turn the negative event into a positive by trying to step up and be more responsible and independent. I felt like I was the next lil Momma when Mom wasn't around to make sure things got done. Because Mom had four kids to raise alone, I started to save money in case of an emergency (for myself so I wouldn't create a financial burden for Mom).

Mom said she relied on Dad not only as a companion, but also for taking care of the financial obligations. Upon his passing, she felt a huge loss for both. What will she do? What stuck with me the most was when Mom said, "There is no day promised to any of us. A person could instantly be out of your life, by death or they could just leave you. You need to cherish and enjoy the time you have with your loved ones. You need to be able to depend on and take care of yourself."

Tara Anne Davis: "I felt a hole and couldn't feel, didn't know how to handle things. I learned about relationships the wrong way. I acted out. My dad died during my foundational years and a piece was missing and I didn't know how to feel about what I didn't understand. Usually a father teaches you unconditional love, but I was seeking relationship in all the wrong places. My dad died young, before I had an understanding of what a good relationship looks like with a man."

Andre Deon Davis: "I was too young to be affected by dad's death. I couldn't comprehend at that time the real impact and was still learning and developing, was resilient and was learning how the world is as it comes. My expectations were open to see what would be. I was impacted more from watching my friend's interactions with their dads at around 12 years old or pre-teen years. I started to really feel the loss much more and during my graduation and marriage as I was thinking about becoming a father."

SUPPORT RESOURCES

After first husband Paul Davis passed:

- Women's prayer group!
- Home church, Family/Friends
- Grief Support group
- Bible Study Fellowship (BSF)
- Community Bible Studies

After my second husband Robbie passed:

- Home church, Family/Friends
- VA Medical Center and to-date provides support for me.
- American Lake VA Dementia unit staff
- Caregiver support groups/Alzheimer's Community Board
- Full Life Care

Scripture:

"Do not be anxious about anything but in every situation pray with thanksgiving."
(Philippians 4:6)

"I can do all things through Christ who gives me strength." *(Philippians 4:13)*

"Those who wait on the Lord shall renew their strength." *(Isaiah 40:31)*

"All things work for the good to them that love the Lord and are called according to His purpose." *(Romans 8:28)*

"I will lift up my eyes to the hills from whence cometh my help." *(Psalm 121)*

"Trust in the Lord and lean not unto thy own understanding but in all thy ways acknowledge Him and He will direct your path." *(Proverbs 3:5)*

"But seek ye first the kingdom of God and His righteousness then all other things shall be added unto thee." *(Matthew 6:33)*

"Cast all your cares on Him and He will direct your path." *(1Peter 5:7)*

"The Lord is my rock, my fortress, my deliverer, my strength in whom I will trust." *(Psalm 18:2)*

"Come unto me all who are weary and burdened and I will give you rest." *(Matthew 11:28)*

Books:

The Bible

The Bible Promise Book

"Death and Dying" by Elizabeth Kubler-Ross

"Jesus Calling" by Sarah Young

"My Name is Hannibal Shanks, A Caregiver's Guide to Alzheimers" by Lela Know Shanks

"When Your Past is Hurting Your Present: Getting Beyond Fears That Hold You Back" by Sue Augustine

"All There Is—Love Stories from Storycorps" by Dave Isay

"Letters from Madelyn: Chronicles of a Caregiver" by Elaine Sanchez

"My Journey into Alzheimer's Disease: Helpful Insights for Family and Friend, A True Story" by Robert Davis

"The 36 Hour Day 4th Edition: A Family Guide for Caring for People with Alzheimer's Disease, Other Dementias and Memory Loss in Later Life" by Nancy L. Mace and Peter V. Rabins

"Relentless: The Power of Your Need to Never Give Up" by John Bevere

"Commanding your Morning: Unleash the Power of God in Your Life" by Cindy Trimm

"I'm Just That Into Me☺: You're The One You've Been Waiting For" by Dayna (Reid) Mason & Jason Andrada

62968056R00060

Made in the USA
Middletown, DE
26 August 2019